ARCHITECTU
A MODERN VIEW

ARCHITECTURE
A MODERN VIEW

RICHARD ROGERS

THAMES AND HUDSON

This is the twenty-second of the annual Walter Neurath Memorial Lectures on subjects reflecting the interests of the founder of Thames and Hudson. The Directors wish to express particular gratitude to the Governors and Master of Birkbeck College, University of London, for their gracious sponsorship of these lectures.

Frontispiece: RRP, Lloyd's of London headquarters. Photo Richard Bryant

Printed and bound in Singapore by C.S. Graphics

I was greatly honoured to be asked to give the twenty-second Walter Neurath Memorial Lecture. A historian would have found it a difficult task successfully to follow such people as Sir Nikolaus Pevsner, Sir Ernst Gombrich, Sir John Summerson and Lord Clark, but for a dyslexic practising architect it was awesome. This is true especially at the present time, when architecture is under such attack and confidence is low. My role was not made any easier by the knowledge that the extraordinary Mr Neurath, a great publisher and connoisseur, had a unique standard of perfection, and reacted with bewildered and eloquent wrath to anything that fell short of it. May I therefore thank Mrs Eva Neurath all the more for her confidence in inviting me to give the lecture. I would also like to thank Ben Rogers for his editorial help and advice.

To illustrate this book, I have used primarily my practice's work, for first and foremost I am a practising architect. I have touched on four inter-related themes: patronage and capitalism, Modernism, Post-Modernism, and the future.

'Architecture immortalizes and glorifies something. Hence there can be no architecture where there is nothing to glorify.' Wittgenstein

The history of architecture should be seen as a history of social and technical invention and not of styles and forms. It is those periods when change quickens and turning points are reached, when innovation is more important than consolidation and the perfecting of style, that interest me most. I prefer Brunelleschi to Michelangelo, Early English Gothic to its decorated successor, Borromini to the historicism that followed.

The last one hundred years has been one of these revolutionary periods, affecting all fields of human endeavour – science, art, economics and politics. We have witnessed an unprecedented and exhilarating explosion of new ideas and technologies, many of which have a profound potential to improve and indeed emancipate our lives. But this very revolution has brought about a political and moral crisis, a crisis which encompasses the globe and which demands a global response.

Despite all our new wealth – material and intellectual - most of the world's inhabitants are denied the opportunity to lead decent lives. The swollen stomachs and shrivelled faces of Third World children, the cold and squalor that our own pensioners have to endure, the increasing number of people who live in boxes and doorways stand as an indictment of a society which has the capacity to eradicate poverty but prefers to turn its back. And beyond the exploitation and injustice which is so central a feature of our civilization looms the prospect of ecological disaster. Our predicament now is that the means to our emancipation threaten our very existence and the existence of other species.

Over the past fifty years, our development has accelerated to the point where if it continues uncontrolled it will destroy humankind. Only by the inauguration of a more conscientious approach, through education, research and above all reflection can we avoid this cataclysm. And avoid it we can, for the problems that face us *are* manageable; there *is* energy, there *is* space and there *are* ways, for the world is immensely rich in natural resources.

Street life outside the Pompidou Centre, Paris

The primitive hut, from Cesariano's Vitruvius, *1521*

Filippo Brunelleschi, dome of Florence Cathedral, 1407

Buckminster Fuller, US Pavilion at Expo, Montreal, 1967

In architecture, turning points in history are reached when ideas and technology meet to force the pace of change; from the secure cave to the mobile hut, from the medieval wall and roof to the floating Renaissance dome, from heavy natural materials to contemporary lightweight synthetics.

The predicament in which we find ourselves has a direct bearing on our appreciation of the successes and failures of modern architecture. For in architecture, as in other areas, an exciting surge in creativity, discovery and invention has been frustrated by the same selfish interests that now sustain global poverty and threaten the environment. Thus, contrary to the myopic views of some leading critics, the ugliness of so much modern architecture is not the responsibility solely of a single body of professionals. The despoliation of our built environment is only a small part of a broader pattern – a pattern in which new advances in ideas and technology are harnessed not to public values but to private interests.

Structural component of the Eiffel Tower, Paris, 1889

If we continue to consider only our individual needs, to be selfish, to specialize rather than to try to understand the universal implication of what we do, or if we retreat into a nostalgic dream of a past that never existed, rather than making best use of the most brilliant modern minds and tools, then our future is bleak, to say the least.

Naum Gabo, Constructed Head, No. 2, *1916*

The 20th century has seen an explosion of new ideas and technologies, but their emancipatory potential has rarely been fulfilled.

Frank Lloyd Wright, Midway Gardens, Chicago, Illinois, 1913

I believe in conservation and in learning from history, but merely copying the past belittles its very integrity. Buckminster Fuller, perhaps the most brilliant environmental philosopher and engineer of this century, wrote: 'Hope in the future is rooted in the memory of the past, for without memory there is no history and no knowledge. No projection of the future can be formed without reference to the past. Past, present and future, memory and prophecy are woven together into one continuous whole. In a clear understanding of the past lies the hope of our future.'

Le Corbusier, Villa Savoye, Poissy, 1929–31

In insisting that the poverty of much of our architecture must be understood as part of a broader pattern, I do not intend to free architects from all responsibility. To begin with, it can be seen with hindsight that some of the assumptions and ideals of the Modern Movement were misguided.

Representing an exciting surge in creativity and invention, the Early Modern Movement was richer and more diverse than its detractors will acknowledge.

Typical back-to-back housing in the north of England, 1930s

Reformist and humanitarian, the Modern Movement evolved as an attempt to remedy the squalor and drabness of the nineteenth-century city, a squalor which we, who have rendered nostalgia an honoured national trait, are apt to forget, but which shocked so many writers of the period. Recall Ruskin's description of the Victorian capital: 'that great foul city of London, rattling, growling, smoking and stinking - a ghastly heap of fermenting brickwork, pouring out poison at every pore!'

However, if the Modernist goal of creating a democratic, affordable architecture to replace the existing slums was commendable, it is perhaps true that in their desire to introduce sunlight, nature and hygiene into the lives of ordinary people, Early Modernists undervalued urban intensity and complexity; they neglected the importance of the interpersonal, spontaneous interaction and exchange which is the very essence of city life.

A reminder that the Modern Movement developed as an attempt to eradicate the squalor and drabness of the 19th-century city.

Katsura Detached Palace, Shoin Building, Kyoto, Japan, early- and mid-17th century

Balthazar Neumann, Kaisersaal, Wurzburg Residenz, 1720–44

Mies van der Rohe, Barcelona Pavilion, 1929

The aim of the Modern Movement was to produce a democratic architecture; the natural simplicity and integrity of Japanese design offered an alternative to the ostentation of its European counterpart.

Piano + Rogers, Pompidou Centre, Paris, 1971–77, piazza activity viewed from the escalator

Not a remote monument but a people's place. Our competition report recommended that the Pompidou Centre be developed as a 'live centre of information covering Paris and beyond . . . a cross between an information orientated computerized Times Square and the British Museum, with the stress on two-way participation between people and activities/exhibits'.

Paternoster Square, London. Left: Paternoster Square development, pre-1939; centre: Paternoster Square, 1957; right: RRP Plan, 1978

In particular, the idea of zoning activities, though appealing at a time when many homes were polluted by factories, has too often resulted in residential and commercial quarters devoid of any vitality or character. With this in mind, many Modernists are now trying to create buildings which provide for a number of overlapping activities. In our design for the Pompidou Centre, and for the National Gallery, for instance, we sought to create centres that could appeal to everyone: children, tourists and locals, students and workers, users and passers-by. We wanted to establish not remote museums but vibrant public meeting places.

Similarly, the Early Modernist tendency to place all buildings in space now seems less attractive than it did in an epoch of chronic overcrowding. Of course, as architects have always known, many important buildings need to stand apart in space. But modern architects have tended to disregard the alternative technique of carving space out of a compact urban fabric. In 1978 we were one of the winners of a competition for the Paternoster Square site, adjacent to St Paul's Cathedral. The existing postwar buildings which were to be demolished consisted of a number of isolated freestanding blocks. In contrast, our plan provided for a solid mass of building out of which space was chiselled in response to focal points, views, movements and entrances. Likewise, in our design for Lloyd's we set out to enhance the narrow medieval street pattern of the city by building over the whole site. This allows the viewer to catch only glimpses of the building, which is therefore designed to be seen in parts.

The Early Modernist architect, like his Classical predecessor, concentrated on buildings as focal points surrounded by space. Medieval buildings, on the other hand, which formed the background to most Classical buildings, consist of a tight matrix of structures in which space is enclosed by buildings. Contemporary architecture should encompass both approaches.

Richard Rogers Partnership, Lloyd's of London headquarters, 1978–86

The mistakes that have characterized the Modern Movement – and doubtless one could add others – have been compounded by the uncritical attitudes of many modern architects. In the struggle to create the movement, mistakes were left unexamined and entered the architectural vocabulary of unquestioning disciples. Indeed it is perhaps the major error of Modernism that it has not learnt fast enough from its failures. Only now are modern architects beginning to think seriously about ways to bring the vitality and complexity back to town and city life.

However, though some Modernist principles are now being discarded or amended, it needs to be emphasized that others continue to animate the best of contemporary architecture. Buildings such as Tadao Ando's housing in Rokko, Japan; Louis Kahn's Kimbell Art Museum, Fort Worth, Texas; or Renzo Piano's Communale Stadium, in Bari, Italy, display an integrity of building materials, an experimental use of new technologies and a sculptural rather than decorative composition which are some of the most enduring features of the Modern Movement.

Lloyd's was designed so as to link together the somewhat oversimplified neighbouring blocks and the more articulated architecture of the past. From a distance the skyline is enriched by the servant towers which place the building within its context.

Louis Kahn, Kimbell Art Museum, Fort Worth, Texas, 1966–72

Tadao Ando, Rokko Housing 1, Rokko Kobe, Hyogo, 1978–83

Renzo Piano, Communale Stadium, Bari, Italy, 1987–90

The best modern buildings continue to be animated by the spirit of Modernism and to display its main features: integrity of building materials, improved environmental conditions, experimental design and sculptural form.

Progressive and extraordinarily diverse at its beginning – much more diverse than its critics will acknowledge – Modernism continues to live on in the most interesting of today's architecture. Despite some of the misconceptions and mistakes that have characterized its history – like any visionary theory it was bound to need revising and adapting – it is nonsense to suggest that the ideas of the Modern Movement can be held *principally* responsible for the despoliation of our cities.

The poverty of much postwar architecture can be traced, on the one hand, to the urgent need to rebuild and expand a severely damaged public infrastructure after six years of war had stretched the economy to breaking point and, on the other, to the growing competitiveness and 'efficiency' of capitalist organizations. This is not to say that there were not many outstanding projects: new towns, schools, hospitals and housing. However, the general picture is one of the public authorities cutting costs and the private sector maximizing profit, and both disregarding architectural quality.

The truth is that the glass boxes, flyovers and tower blocks of the postwar years are not the legacy of a fallacious aesthetic dogma nor testimony to the arrogance of Britain's architects. They represent something far more real and disturbing: the fact that one of the most important aspects of our public life – our architecture – has been sacrificed to the private interests of the market and the short-sighted economies of public officials.

One cannot deny that architects have played an important role in this fiasco. Not because they were Modernists, but because many of them have been too ready to collude with their clients in the view that architecture is just another profitable business with no bearing on the public at large. I have no wish to excuse those architects who have designed the cheap, second-rate

RRP, Iikura office building, Tokyo, 1987

Constructivism, Cubism and Futurism celebrated the dynamic spirit of Modernism and the potential of the machine. All three have greatly interested and influenced us.

developments, but blaming them alone conceals the extent to which the large corporations, the developers and the government are deeply implicated.

Jacob Tchernykhov, Industrial Project, Leningrad, 1933

RRP, GRC Headquarters, Lyon. Offices, shops, hotel and residential, 1990

RRP, Coin Street Development, South Bank, London, 1979–83. Service tower

Architects cannot work in a vacuum; unlike other artists they are totally dependent on a site, a brief and finance. Good architecture, in this age as in any other, is born of an enlightened client, generous financing and a public-minded brief. It is the absence of precisely this sense of public pride and patronage rather than the alleged inhumanity of Modernism that has been the most pernicious factor at work in British architecture. Clients in both the public and private sphere have, generally speaking, shown an extraordinary insensitivity to the quality of our architectural environment; a look at the 'enterprise zones' of the London Docklands and elsewhere, where most planning restrictions have been lifted, shows only too clearly that a philistine commercialism is still the order of the day.

There is every reason to believe that all periods produce some good architects and today clients can choose architects from anywhere in the world. As it is, there are a handful of British architects, such as James Stirling, Sir Norman Foster, Sir Denys Lasdun, Michael Hopkins and Nicholas Grimshaw, who are recognized internationally as among the finest in the world, although, in the case of the first two, one has to go abroad to see the best examples of their work.

No one blames the artist if a museum has a bad collection, or the author if a library has a bad selection. As long as there are good painters and writers the blame must fall on those responsible for selection. The same is true regarding architecture.

What place has there been, however, for a civic-minded patronage in the ethical climate of the last decade? The latest stage of capitalism, as exemplified in the policies pursued by Margaret Thatcher and Ronald Reagan, confesses that money and profit are ends in themselves and no longer a means to achieve an end.

This argument is based on the principle that financial wealth, once established among the rich, will trickle down and generally benefit all classes. Personally I see no sign of this; on the contrary, Thatcherism seems a confirmation of the 'deluge up' rather than the 'trickle down' theory.

'Form follows profit' is the aesthetic principle of our times. Thus, design skill is measured today by the architect's ability to build the largest possible enclosure for the smallest investment in the quickest time. The factors that now determine the design of a building are maximum economic efficiency in terms of rentable space to gross space, wall to floor ratios and minimum storey height. The result is invariably a single-activity building in the form of a thin-skinned box – a shopping centre, an office building or a block of flats – with no unprofitable public spaces, no expressive or innovative structural features and certainly no room to celebrate the art of Architecture. Arcades, gardens and balconies, even recessed windows, impinge on rentable space and are deemed incompatible with the profit principle. And because developers and their shareholders want a quick return on their investment – the horizons of stockbrokers and accountants do not extend to posterity – the cheapest materials must be used. Some clients refuse to plant even trees; no acorn will increase the rentable value of a property, and no investor, we are told, will wait for an oak.

Most contemporary architecture is therefore the product of stark economic forces rather than the work of a designer; it represents the logical product of a society which sees the environment in terms of profit. All developers are in competition; any developer who puts long-term interests first is likely to lose out and benefit his less responsible competitors, opening up his company to a takeover and asset stripping. Only if the government steps in and legislates for the public good can quality be achieved.

Offices, Hammersmith Road, London, 1989

The brilliant, single-minded efficiency of modern business is endangering both our culture and our universe. I wish to stress that maximum profit, as shown by the bottom line of a balance sheet, presented annually to shareholders, where buildings are written off over ten years, has little to do with the creation of a quality orientated society.

A familiar model: a building designed on the principle 'form follows profit' – maximum lettable space for the least capital investment.

The architect's vocation has been reduced to designing 'machines for making investments in' and short-term investments at that. A prominent lawyer, speaking in 1989 at the American Institute of Architecture, encapsulated the attitude of most contemporary clients: 'You will deliver service to us, the way we want, or we will take the business elsewhere. Only in this way will you survive in the nineties.'

If clients view the commissioning of an architect exclusively on these terms – as nothing more than a business venture – then the public clamour for architects to improve their standards is bound to be futile. The problem concerns the standard of demand rather than supply. There has been much talk of improving architectural education, but this type of measure is likely to fall at the same hurdle. It does not matter how well trained architects are, if the client chooses the one most willing to design for profit rather than beauty.

My own experience has taught me that enlightened and committed clients are as crucial a part of the 'design team' as architects and engineers. There is no way that architects can design squares, parks or buildings of any quality without their patronage and direction. For example, with a responsible client such as Lloyd's, our contact with its Chairman, Head of Development, board of directors and numerous user committees was on literally a day to day basis. A wide range of options was presented and full-scale models of pieces of the building were constructed for Lloyd's approval. In cases such as this, the finished building reflects the dedication and sensitivity of the client just as much as the contribution of the architect.

RRP, Lloyd's of London headquarters, 1978–86

Architecture is teamwork in which the client plays a major role. Lloyd's reflects the dedication and sensitivity of the client just as much as the contribution of the architect.

Fortunately, there are other firms and political authorities who, like Lloyd's, continue to display a generous sense of public patronage. At King's Cross, Stuart Lipton and Godfrey Bradman are endeavouring to create an urban park worthy of our Georgian predecessors. (It is startling to realize that if this project sees the light of day it will be the first large park to have been built in central London this century.) The Sainsburys are responsible for Sir Norman Foster's museum at the University of East Anglia and for Robert Venturi's new wing of the National Gallery. And, despite drastic cuts in construction by local authorities, Hampshire County Council has commissioned some outstanding designs. But these scattered instances of enlightened commissions and others like them do not undermine my point. Rather, by demonstrating the possibility of architectural patronage, they serve only to establish its general paucity.

Norman Foster, masterplan for the King's Cross Development, London, 1989

The public realm is being eroded by individual greed. The primary role of cities is for the meeting of people, but though large urban parks, squares and boulevards were a feature of 18th- and 19th-century urban planning, London has not had a comparable public space this century.

Parthenon, Athens

Post-Modernism developed as a reaction to the limitations and errors of Early Modernism and its inability either to learn from its mistakes or to develop fast enough to meet changing needs. However, if Post-Modernism originally represented a protest against the monotony and alienating character of much modern, in particular International Style, architecture, it has rapidly become the superficial aesthetic of shoddy commercial design. Its sympathy for historicism has degenerated all too often into a shallow decoration, a self-indulgent playing with symbols, which has no integral relation to the functions of the building, but succeeds in disguising its fundamental poverty. If Post-Modernist publications tend to dwell on elevations, it is because plan and section – the stuff of the best modern architecture – have been entirely given over to the maximization of rentable space.

Ricardo Bofill, Les Espaces d'Abraxas, Marne la Vallée, 1983

Classical proportion is based on mathematical formulae, such as the diameter of a column, which is the module that governs the form of the building. Post-Modernism has all too often degenerated into a shallow decoration, with no real affinities with the Classical order it professes to admire.

Modern architecture arose from a belief in the potential quality of modern society – in its capacity to provide a high standard of shelter and welfare for people. But whereas Early Modernists sought to evolve new forms and building types appropriate for an industrial democratic society, their Post-Modernist successors have been reduced to tinkering with cornices and pediments. Post-Modern buildings are now decorated in pretty costumes: Neo-Classical, Gothic, Egyptian or Gypsy Vernacular.

Post-Modernism, obsessed with money and fashion, has not produced rigorous design or a better environment, for it cannot offer solutions to a world in need of an architecture which deals with the lack of public space, with the greening of the environment, with shelter for the less fortunate, with machines, flexibility and change. Aesthetics dominate ethics; the homeless, the unemployed, the schizophrenic wander in an ever-increasing hostile environment, adding to social tensions. The aesthetics of prettiness and the heritage industry are not the solution. The problem is not style but quality, not aesthetics but ethics.

The Post Modernist architect rummages in the dustbin of history, picking out Egyptian, Classical, Art Deco and Bauhaus ideas.
Cartoon of Philip Johnson, Financial Times, 22.12.1986

The failure to accord any sort of value to our civic life is nowhere more evident than in British cities. There is apparently no modern equivalent to the sense of patronage which created the great parks, the market places, the fountains and the majestic tree-lined avenues of the Georgian epoch.

The architect is in danger of becoming a decorator of boxes. Neo-Classical, Gothic, Egyptian or Gypsy Vernacular motifs are being applied like a pretty label to a tin of beans.

RRP, National Gallery Extension, 1982. Model

RRP, National Gallery Extension. Model: Plan of Trafalgar Square showing the four focal points

RRP, National Gallery Extension. South elevation to Trafalgar Square

There are important visual, technical and social lessons to be learnt from the past, but merely copying the outward forms belittles history. For example, to strengthen the geometry in our proposals for the extension to the National Gallery, Trafalgar Square, we proposed a third tower to complete a triangle, whose other two corners are Nelson's Column and the spire of St Martin-in-the-Fields. This also helps frame the central entrance to the National Gallery.

Indeed, while British cities are now among the most neglected in Europe, cities on the Continent are constantly in the process of being repaired and enriched. From Helsinki to Naples, rush-hour traffic is being re-routed away from city centres. But in London, the 'people's places' – Trafalgar Square, Piccadilly Circus, Oxford Circus, Marble Arch, Hyde Park Corner, Parliament Square – are being allowed to become nothing more than hazardous and congested roundabouts.

For every new public building in France – and there are many – the government has stipulated that a competition must be held, in which design is a prime consideration. A special government commission chaired by a senior architect directly accountable to the minister responsible for architecture oversees the competition system. Furthermore, following President Mitterand's example in Paris of Les Grands Projets, nearly every city mayor is involved in competitions, preparing strategies for the replanning of their city and the building of public edifices. This is subsidized by central and local government. My own practice has been involved in these planning exercises in some ten French cities, and I can assure you that there is absolutely nothing comparable to them in Britain.

Over the past fifteen years an unbelievable change has taken place in France. When in 1971 Renzo Piano and I won the competition for the Pompidou Centre, the French chairman of the jury advised us not to employ French architects, due to their poor standards. Today, through direct government intervention, France has probably the best younger generation of architects whereas Britain's younger architects have had little chance to build. Where is the work of Alsop, Hadid, Hordon, Richie or Wilson?

Vision and large-scale co-ordination are essential to successful planning. A national plan aimed at a more beautiful environment should be drawn up, stipulating standards and giving planners the right to insist on those standards so that planning permission becomes a positive rather than a negative tool. Public authorities must be willing, at the very least, to insert demanding environmental standards into the planning laws, making balconies, parks and cultural amenities as obligatory as fire escapes. In France, local and national governments generally sell land at a fixed price so that developers compete on the quality of design. In Britain, the highest bidder wins, and the highest bid is paid for by the slashing of construction costs and quality.

In 1986, in our scheme 'London As It Could Be', part of the exhibition 'New Architecture: Foster, Rogers, Stirling' at the Royal Academy, we demonstrated how the centre of London could be transformed by pedestrianizing and linking together some

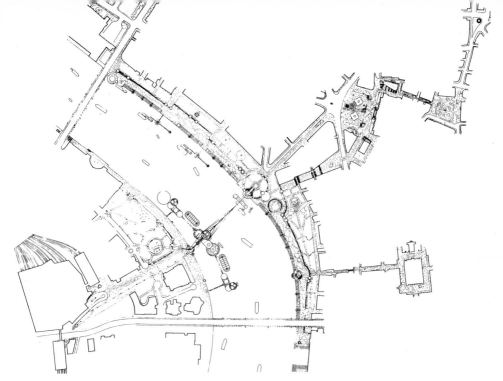

RRP, London As It Could Be, 1986. Plan linking Leicester Square to Waterloo and Vauxhall Bridge to Blackfriars

of its most important spaces. We recommended the sinking of the noisy road along the embankment from Westminster to Blackfriars, thereby connecting many little existing pockets of green space and thus establishing a linear park along the Thames. In the other direction we recommended the creation of a pedestrian route linking Leicester Square and Trafalgar Square with the South Bank and Waterloo Station. This involved the building of a pedestrian bridge and a number of floating islands.

Aerial view of site

Major public benefits could be achieved by weaving together and strengthening the existing public realm.

Sir William Chambers, Somerset House, 1776. Watergate

Without demolishing any old buildings of note, this scheme would have made the centre of London a dramatically more humane place to live and work in; it would have given the city back its heart. But under the present circumstances a project like this can never hope to be realized. It would have to secure the approval of more than fifty public authorities and advisory bodies, some of which, like Lambeth and Westminster, refuse on principle to co-operate on any matter. Once again, British cities are uniquely deprived; London is alone among the capitals of Europe in having no public body with the specific responsibility of promoting and overseeing projects which are intended to affect the civic life of the city as a whole.

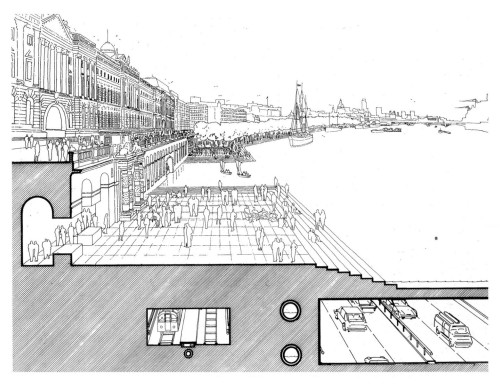

RRP, London As It Could Be. New linear park. Traffic would be contained in a tunnel under the river

Prince Charles and his followers have been praised for focusing attention on the wretched nature of many British townscapes and landscapes. But by limiting their attack to a question of superficial style, and by blaming architects alone, these critics have avoided finding any fault with the political and financial reality, the fact that architectural patronage and urban planning are in the hands of commercial and political bodies for whom quality appears to be a very low priority. If these critics believe that it would overstep acceptable bounds if they were to take on the true culprits, they should never have started their attack, for to go thus far and no further leaves them open to the criticism that they are poorly informed and lacking in courage.

The imposing watergate of Somerset House now fronts a 4-lane motorway which creates an almost impenetrable barrier to the river. By sinking the highway, a major south-facing riverside linear park, lined with cafés, restaurants, shops and galleries, can be created without the demolition of a single building.

31

John Hawkshaw, Hungerford Railway Bridge, 1863

RRP, London As It Could Be. Model of proposed new bridge

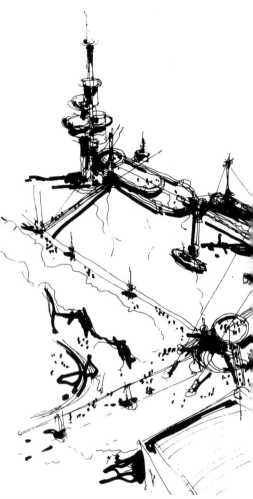

RRP, London As It Could Be. Sketch of proposed bridge

The noisy and hideous Hungerford Railway Bridge with its adjoining footpath is replaced by a new suspension bridge and a number of floating islands containing public amenities such as museums and restaurants.

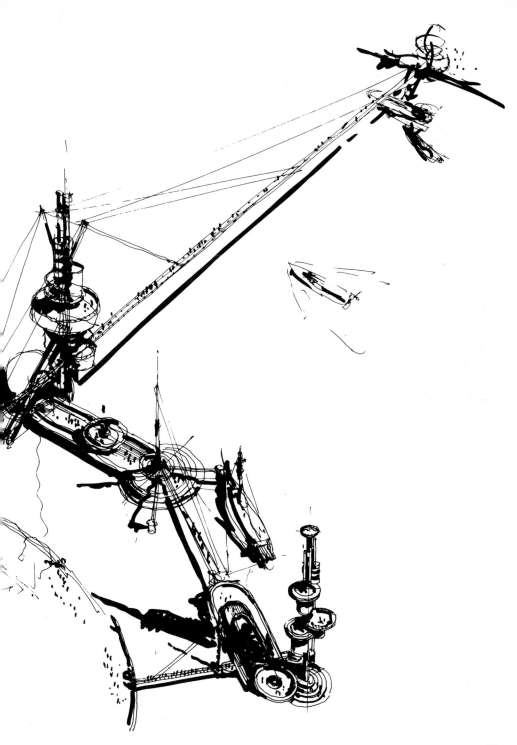

RRP, London As It Could Be. Proposed pedestrian bridge with monorail shuttle underneath

RRP, London As It Could Be. Proposed new piazza outside the National Gallery

Existing piazza

Trafalgar Square – 'the heart of an Empire' – is an alienating roundabout devoid of any public activities. Pall Mall east could be closed by placing a small roundabout to the south, thereby opening up Trafalgar Square to the public and creating a wonderful new high level piazza outside the National Gallery.

Cathedral of Notre Dame, Paris, c. 1163–1250

Piano + Rogers, Pompidou Centre. The bracket: a 10-ton steel casting, 8.2m long

From its beginning, modern architecture, like its Classical forerunners, has always been concerned to incorporate new technology into its designs. Its most successful buildings have celebrated the technology with which they are built and have been filled with a sense of innovation and exploration.

This technological adventurousness has provoked the criticism that modern buildings are incapable of harmonizing with their older surroundings. But the fact is that all significant architectural movements have been innovative and indeed revolutionary in their time, with the result that some of the most beautiful architectural compositions in the world emerge precisely from the juxtaposition of great buildings of very different styles clearly and courageously relating through time. St Mark's Square in Venice or the Piazza Signoria in Florence are good illustrations.

The buildings of all epochs have celebrated the technology with which they were built. The steel framework of the Pompidou Centre gives order and flexibility of use. The double-span flying buttresses of Notre Dame enable the Gothic cathedral to reach up to God.

King's College, Cambridge. Centre: King's College Chapel, 1446–1515; right: James Gibbs, Fellows' Building, 1723–29

Perhaps the very best example of individually beautiful but totally contrasting designs creating a harmonious whole is provided by that wonderful cluster of buildings at King's College, Cambridge. The great Gothic chapel once stood isolated in a meadow until enlightened patrons had the courage to change what must have appeared at the time to have been a perfect situation. Today we see medieval and Classical buildings adjoining the Gothic chapel creating one of the most sublime vistas in England.

Harmony achieved through the juxtaposition of buildings of different epochs. It is disturbing to realize that had today's conservative architectural climate prevailed, the later buildings in King's College, Cambridge, would never have received planning permission. They would have been considered 'unsympathetic', too modern, and detracting from an already perfect situation.

What is true of the modern buildings of the past is equally true of the most innovative buildings of the present. One has only to think of Mies van der Rohe's Seagram Building in New York, or, more recently still, the I. M. Pei & Partners pyramid for the Louvre, to see that modern architecture can respond to an urban context in a manner that has never been surpassed.

Modern architecture is rich in different theories and solutions, from underground cities by architects such as Paolo Soleri in Arizona, to work by Britain's Future Systems Architects for NASA space labs, via James Stirling and Michael Wilford's Staatsgalerie in Stuttgart and Norman Foster's Hongkong and Shanghai Bank.

I.M. Pei & Partners, proposed extension to the National Gallery, London, 1981

I.M. Pei & Partners, The Grand Louvre, Paris, completed 1989

The design for the Louvre by I.M. Pei & Partners is an excellent example of a modern building contrasting harmoniously with its surroundings. The historicist design for the National Gallery extension, by the same firm, would have done much less to enhance Trafalgar Square but says a great deal about the American architect's view of French and British tastes.

RRP, refurbished interior, Billingsgate Fish Market, London, 1986–89

Sir Horace Jones, Billingsgate Fish Market, 1875

RRP, refurbished interior, Billingsgate Fish Market

RRP, refurbished Billingsgate Fish Market with Lloyd's in the background

In our conversion of Billingsgate Fish Market into a banking centre, we sought harmony of modern with old in a single building. We restored the old building to its original condition, but used the most modern designs when it came to inserting new parts.

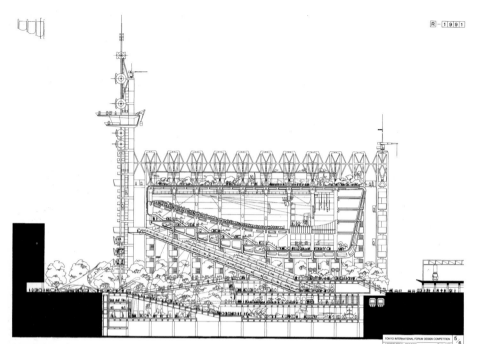

RRP, Tokyo International Forum Design Competition, 1989. Longitudinal section

I believe in the rich potential of science and technology. Aesthetically one can do what one wants with technology, for it is a tool and not an end, but we ignore it at our peril, for without it we cannot achieve our potential. For example, my practice's design for the Tokyo Forum competition is based on the development of an urban people's meeting place. A filigree steel structure supports three suspended shining steel shells which contain the auditorium. On their roofs are gardens and reception facilities. The ground level consists of three linked piazzas partially sheltered by the overhead auditoriums. On the ground are exhibition spaces, information centres, studios, shops and a restaurant. Great glazed escalators take millions of people through the open space between the piazzas and air-based activities.

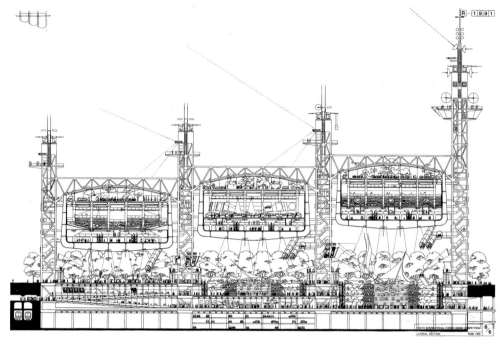

RRP, Tokyo International Forum Design Competition. Lateral section

New technological developments offer architects an extraordinary opportunity to evolve new forms and materials. The computer, micro-chip, transputer, bio-technology and solid state chemistry could lead to an enhanced environment, including more rather than less individual control and fewer uniform spaces. Architects and engineers such as Buckminster Fuller, Archigram, Cedric Price, John Johansen and Jan Kaplicky have explored the avenues opened up by these developments.

The Tokyo Forum is designed as a public meeting place. Modern technology has allowed us to develop a new range of spaces, experiences and activities expressed by new forms. Social concept, technology and form are inseparable.

RRP, Tokyo International Forum Design Competition, 1989

I believe in the rich potential of science and technology. Aesthetically one can do what one wants with technology, for it is a tool and not an end, but we ignore it at our peril, for without it we cannot achieve our potential.

I am searching for an architecture which will express and celebrate the ever-quickening speed of social, technical, political and economic change; an architecture of permanence and transformation where urban vitality and economic dynamics can take place, reflecting the changing and overlapping of functions; building as a form of controlled randomness which can respond to complex situations and relationships. Such architecture can be partially achieved by the zoning of buildings into long-life served and short-life servant activities.

Team 4, Reliance Controls Electronics Factory, Swindon, Wiltshire, 1967. Before

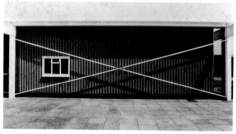

And after

The creation of an architecture which incorporates the new technologies entails breaking away from the platonic idea of a static world, expressed by the perfect finite object to which nothing can be added or taken away, a concept which has dominated architecture since its beginning. Instead of Schelling's description of architecture as frozen music, we are looking for an architecture more like some modern music, jazz or poetry, where improvisation plays a part, an indeterminate architecture containing both permanence and transformation.

Reliance Controls included many of the ideas developed in future work. The windows inserted after completion destroyed the finite platonic quality of the building. This led to the search for an indeterminate form of architecture which could absorb some change. The Pompidou Centre was the first building to incorporate these developments.

Piano + Rogers, Pompidou Centre, Paris, 1971–77. Structural rose connection

Piano + Rogers, Pompidou Centre, Paris, 1971–77. Piazza elevation

The Pompidou Centre incorporated the concept of indeterminacy: certain parts of the building can be added or removed without destroying the balance of the whole.

Overleaf: RRP, Lloyd's of London headquarters. Atrium. Left: looking down;
right: looking up

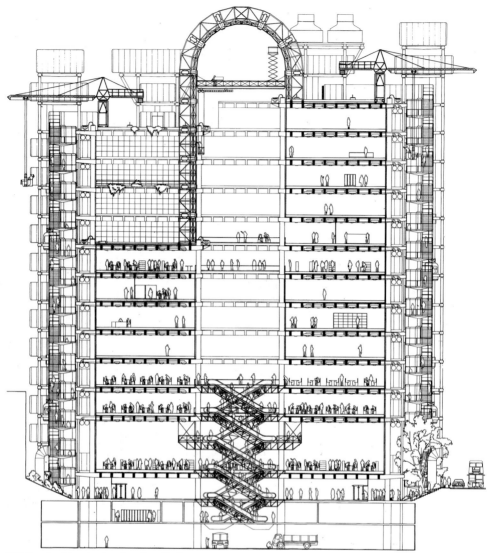

RRP, Lloyd's of London headquarters. Section

Buildings should not constrain the everchanging nature of the institutions they house. Lloyd's had already outgrown three buildings this century. The brief demanded 'flexibility to meet changing needs well into the next century', implying not only easily adaptable interiors but a form organized so that parts could be added or removed without loss of design integrity.

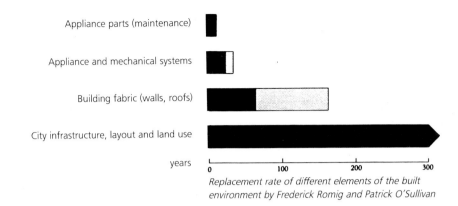

Appliance parts (maintenance)

Appliance and mechanical systems

Building fabric (walls, roofs)

City infrastructure, layout and land use

years

| 0 | 100 | 200 | 300 |

Replacement rate of different elements of the built environment by Frederick Romig and Patrick O'Sullivan

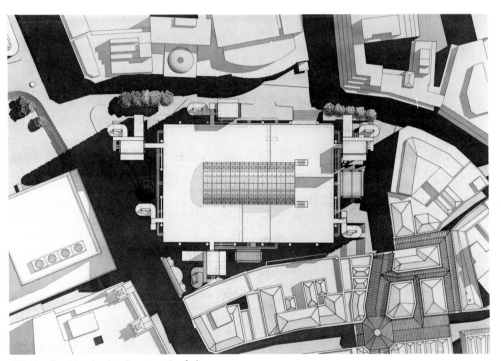

RRP, Lloyd's of London headquarters. Roof plan

If one can access and change short-life parts of a building, its total lifespan can be extended. Lloyd's is clearly divided into a long-life central zone housing people and a short-life external zone containing technology.

RRP, INMOS, 1982. Night view of circulation spire

In the case of Britain's first microchip factory – INMOS – technology drives the design. Three-quarters of its budget and the larger part of its volume are devoted to constantly changing mechanical services.

RRP, INMOS. General view of west elevation

RRP, perspex model of the European Court of Human Rights, Strasbourg, begun 1989

RRP, perspex model of the European Court of Human Rights. Aerial view

With the European Court of Human Rights, technological considerations were secondary. Our design was generated by the public nature of the building, its symbolic importance and its situation adjacent to a curve on a river.

The best buildings of the future, for example, will interact dynamically with the climate in order better to meet the users' needs and make optimum use of energy. More like robots than temples, these apparitions with their chameleon-like surfaces insist that we rethink yet again the art of building. Architecture will no longer be a question of mass and volume but of lightweight structures whose superimposed transparent layers will create form so that constructions will become dematerialized.

To date – and here I include Early Modernism – architectural concepts have been founded on linear, static, hierarchical and mechanical order. Today we know that design based on linear reasoning must be superseded by an open-ended architecture of overlapping systems. This 'systems' approach allows us to appreciate the world as an indivisible whole; we are, in architecture, as in other fields, approaching a holistic ecological view of the globe and the way we live on it.

In architecture, invisible micro-electronics and bio-technology are replacing industrial mechanical systems. We shall soon be living in a world so non-mechanical that buildings such as our Lloyd's of London, which is generally considered too innovative, will seem outdated and look old-fashioned.

Chameleon

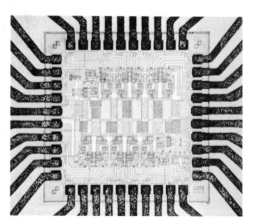

Micro-chip

Technology will offer us more control rather than less. The buildings of the future will be more like robots than temples. Like chameleons, they will adapt to their environment.

Future Systems Architects, Acropolis Museum Competition, 1990

Future architecture will be animated by a holistic ecological view of the globe. Non-mechanical, it will be fluid, seamless and self-regulating, programmed by electronic and bio-technical means to interact with the user and the climate. Future Systems Architects' free-form lightweight monocock museum structure is enclosed by an everchanging polychromatic glass which responds to the climate.

Buildings, the city and its citizens will be one inseparable organism sheltered by a perfectly fitting, ever-changing framework. Posts, beams, panels and other structural elements will be replaced by a seamless continuity. These mobile, changing robots will possess many of the characteristics of living systems, interacting and self-regulating, constantly adjusting through electronic and bio-technological self-programming. Man, shelter, food, work and leisure will be connected and mutually dependent so that an ecological symbiosis will be achieved.

Present day concern for single objects will be replaced by concern for relationships. Shelters will no longer be static objects, but dynamic frameworks. Accommodation will be responsive, ever-changing and ever-adjusting. Cities of the future will no longer be zoned as today in isolated one-activity ghettos; rather, they will resemble the more richly layered cities of the past. Living, work, shopping, learning and leisure will overlap and be housed in continuous, varied and changing structures.

In the case of architectural structures, responsive systems, acting much like muscles flexing in a body, will reduce mass to a minimum by shifting loads and forces with the aid of an electronic nervous system which will sense environmental changes and register individual needs.

Today, automatic pilots in aeroplanes can monitor all control functions and environmental parameters many times a second, continuously adapting and modifying the aircraft control systems to achieve optimal flight and passenger comfort. The future is here, but its impact on architecture is only just beginning to be felt.

Michael Davies, one of my partners, has described the experience of living in a responsive building of the future:

Look up at a spectrum-washed envelope, whose surface is a map of its instantaneous performance, stealing energy from the air with an iridescent shrug, rippling its photo-grids as a cloud runs across the sun, a wall which, as the night chill falls, fluffs up its feathers and, turning white on its north face and blue on the south, closes its eyes but not without remembering to pump a little glow down to the night porter, clear a view-patch for the lovers on the south side of level 22 and so turn 12 percent silver just before dawn.

It is not popular to link the economy and consumption with culture, and to suggest that today it is the accounting system that dictates the Arts. Yet I firmly believe that to achieve a new cultural enlightenment, one which includes architecture, it will be necessary to redefine the balance between capital, labour, the planet and its poor.

Red Arrows flying over the pyramids, Egypt

The collapse of Eastern European communism and the reforms set up by President Gorbachev offer the leading nations the chance to assess environmental and political priorities in humanistic terms. The many billions spent on arms can now be redirected to creating a more just and beautiful world, in which a civic architecture takes its place alongside education, anti-pollution, health and food as priorities. We stand, potentially, at the beginning of a new age of enlightenment, no longer on the scale of Ancient Greece, but encompassing the whole planet.

From pyramids to fighter jets – incredible advances in technology, today much of it squandered on armaments.

Thermal map of the world

I confess my opposition to our present
exploitative economic system and my faith
and unshaken conviction that a global
community in which art and science are
harnessed to serve the common good would
represent the most beautiful and enlight-
ening achievement of the human spirit.

**The challenge that faces us is to overcome the hiatus that exists between
technological and ethical achievement. Advances in technology mean that
for the first time we stand potentially at the dawn of a new age of global
enlightenment.**

Sources of illustrations

The majority of the photographs used in this book are from the collection of Richard Rogers Partnership which has made every effort to establish the copyright holder in each case. Other sources of illustrations are as follows:

Arcaid/Brecht-Einzig: p. 14; Arcaid/Richard Bryant: pp. 16, 23; Archimedia, photo Masaaki Sekiya: p. 18; Architectural Association: p. 12; photo Peter Cook: p. 51; photos Richard Davies: pp. 32, 59; photo John Donat: p. 27 top; *Financial Times*: p. 26; Architects – Foster Associates: p. 24; photo Janet Gill: p. 50; photo Serge Hambourg: pp. 38–39; photo Tina Himsley: p. 21; Hulton Picture Company: pp. 37, 40 bottom left; photos Ken Kirkwood: pp. 54, 55; London Zoo: p. 58 top; photo Nick Macrae: p. 32 top; National Gallery, London: p. 38 left; photos Eamonn O'Mahony: p. 40 top and bottom right, p. 41; Renzo Piano Architecture/Building Workshop, photo Berenzo Gardin: p. 17 bottom; photo Paul Wakefield: pp. 48–49.

The publishers would like to thank those architects who supplied illustrations of their work.

Clown sitting on the cross bracing at the Pompidou Centre